Just
Grandma
and Me

The fill-in, tear-out,
fold-up book of
fun for girls and
their grandmas

★American Girl®

Published by American Girl Publishing, Inc.
Copyright © 2011 by American Girl, LLC

Questions or comments? Call 1-800-845-0005, visit our Web site at americangirl.com,
or write to Customer Service, American Girl, 8400 Fairway Place, Middleton, WI 53562-0497.

Printed in China
11 12 13 14 15 16 LEO 10 9 8 7 6 5 4 3 2 1

Editorial Development: Trula Magruder, Erin Falligant
Art Direction & Design: Gretchen Becker
Production: Jeannette Bailey, Sarah Boecher, Tami Kepler, Judith Lary
Illustrations: Stacy Peterson

Photography: p. 4—© iStockphoto/salihguler (smelling); p. 9—© iStockphoto/alekcey
(four multi-colored cups); p. 13—© iStockphoto/bibikoff (slippers); p. 20—© iStockphoto/
monkeybusinessimages (grandmother with granddaughter); p. 33—© American Girl/Travis Mancl
(brag box); p. 48—© iStockphoto/diane39 (picnic basket); p. 51—© iStockphoto/Imo (gerberas
in XXXL); p. 51—© iStockphoto/pjohnson1 (jelly beans); p. 53—© iStockphoto/totallyjamie
(women's shoes); p. 53—© iStockphoto/JackJelly (tomato soup); p. 55—© iStockphoto/A_Carina
(cameo gem); p. 59—© American Girl/Radlund Studios (petite perfumes); p. 74—© iStockphoto/
ajt (stack of books); p. 81—© iStockphoto/mstay (pencil me in)

Dear Reader,

You can turn the time you spend with your grandma into long-lasting memories—and this book will help!

Use the quizzes to learn more about each other. Make a collection of crafts together. And explore fun ideas on how to stay connected—even if you live many miles apart. You'll even find notes, cooking labels, and coupons to pull out and share.

So make a date with your grandma, and then make it great!

Your friends at American Girl

This or That

Check off the things you like best, and ask your grandma to do the same. How many answers do you have in common?

Tear out and fill out the following lists—one for you and one for your grandma!

Me

- ☐ radio   or   ☐ CDs
- ☐ pink   or   ☐ purple
- ☐ pancakes   or   ☐ waffles
- ☐ winter   or   ☐ summer
- ☐ comedy   or   ☐ drama
- ☐ laptop   or   ☐ desktop
- ☐ books   or   ☐ magazines
- ☐ kisses   or   ☐ hugs
- ☐ bath   or   ☐ shower
- ☐ cheddar cheese   or   ☐ American cheese
- ☐ horse show   or   ☐ dog show
- ☐ cake   or   ☐ pie
- ☐ flowers   or   ☐ chocolates
- ☐ necklace   or   ☐ bracelet
- ☐ potato chips   or   ☐ popcorn

Grandma

- ❑ radio   or   ❑ CDs
- ❑ pink   or   ❑ purple
- ❑ pancakes   or   ❑ waffles
- ❑ winter   or   ❑ summer
- ❑ comedy   or   ❑ drama
- ❑ laptop   or   ❑ desktop
- ❑ books   or   ❑ magazines
- ❑ kisses   or   ❑ hugs
- ❑ bath   or   ❑ shower
- ❑ cheddar cheese   or   ❑ American cheese
- ❑ horse show   or   ❑ dog show
- ❑ cake   or   ❑ pie
- ❑ flowers   or   ❑ chocolates
- ❑ necklace   or   ❑ bracelet
- ❑ potato chips   or   ❑ popcorn

Tea for Two

Plan a private tea party for you and your grandma. Dress up. Serve finger foods and scones. Or try out a charming restaurant. Just don't forget the tea!

Detail a Day

Shorten the distance between you and your grandma by updating her on a single day in your life. Describe breakfast. Chat about class. And fill her in on a favorite friend. Send one postcard about a school day and one about a weekend.

Tear out these cards, fill them out, and mail them. Remember stamps!

To: _____

_____

_____

↳School day

Weekend↴

To: _____

_____

_____

Special Sleepover

Plan a slumber party with your grandma! See if you can stay over at her house—without your mom or dad. Watch a movie, do each other's hair, eat snacks, and work through some of the pages in this book.

Who Knows Best?

You and your grandmother have at least one thing in common—your mom or dad! But how well do you really know your parent? Team up with your grandma to answer the questions shown at right. (If you can't agree, write down both answers.) Then pass the duplicate page to your mom or dad to fill out. Now compare the pages. How well did you and your grandma do? What did you learn?

Tear out the following question sheets. You and your grandma will share one, and you'll give one to your mother or father.

For You & Your Grandma

Grandma and I think that Mom or Dad . . .

• likes to relax here:

_____

• loves to prepare this meal:

_____

• wishes she/he never had to do this chore again:

_____

_____

• likes to order this in restaurants:

_____

• loves this type of movie:

_____

• wishes she/he had more free time to do this:

_____

_____

• likes this fashion item when she/he dresses up:

_____

• loves this treat when she/he splurges:

_____

• wishes she/he had this dream job:

_____

_____

• likes this pizza topping:

_____

• loves to sing this song:

_____

• wishes she/he had enough money to do this:

_____

_____

For Mom or Dad

I really . . .

- like to relax here:

- love to prepare this meal:

- wish I never had to do this chore again:

- like to order this in restaurants:

- love this type of movie:

- wish I had more free time to do this:

- like this fashion item when I dress up:

- love this treat when I splurge:

- wish I had this dream job:

- like this pizza topping:

- love to sing this song:

- wish I had enough money to do this:

Seesaw Stories

Read one of these story starters out loud to your grandma. Take turns adding sentences to the story until one of you declares "the end."

 (Your name here) read the note her grandma had left for her on the table. "Not again, Grandma," she moaned and walked out the door to . . .

 (Your name here) opened the door to her grandmother's house and screamed. "Grandma! How in the world did you get a (fill in the blank) in here?"

(Your name here)'s grandmother said. "I've just won the lottery! Now you and I will be able to . . ."

 "We can solve this mystery," (your name here)'s grandma said. "We just need to put our heads together. Now who'd take our (fill in the blank)?"

In (your name here)'s dream, she and her grandma had odd superpowers. She could (fill in the blank) and her grandma could (fill in the blank)!

Two of a Kind

Add a little flair to a pair of frames. Punch out the frames and the hearts and flowers art on the following pages. Use Glue Dots to attach the art pieces to each frame. Put a copy of the same photo of the two of you in each frame. Keep one and give one to your grandmother.

Find or have someone take a photo of you with your grandma,
and make two prints. Tape one print behind this window and
one behind the window on the following page. Slide each print
into a 5-by-7-inch picture frame.

you & me

Hearts Apart

Keep your faraway grandma
close to your heart by
• mailing a doodle journal
back and forth.
• writing a story together
by e-mail.
• playing a word game online.

Question
Concentration

Here's a winning way to get to know your grandma better. Lay the concentration cards facedown on a table. You each take turns flipping over two cards. If the cards don't match, turn them back facedown. If they do match, you get to ask your opponent the question shown on the cards. Keep the pairs you match. In the end, the one with the most cards—and the most answers!—wins.

Tear out the concentration cards on the following pages. Shuffle the cards before playing.

What's your favorite **outdoor activity?**	What's your favorite **outdoor activity?**	What **three places** on the planet would you most like to visit?	What **three places** on the planet would you most like to visit?
What's one item that **means a lot** to you? Explain why.	What's one item that **means a lot** to you? Explain why.	If you were in a singing competition, what **song would you sing?**	If you were in a singing competition, what **song would you sing?**
What is one difference between your **generation** and mine?	What is one difference between your **generation** and mine?	If you got **$1,000**, what would you do with it?	If you got **$1,000**, what would you do with it?
What person do you **admire most?** Why?	What person do you **admire most?** Why?	What **silly thing** do you do when no one's looking?	What **silly thing** do you do when no one's looking?
What do you think is the **greatest invention** ever?	What do you think is the **greatest invention** ever?	Is there **one place** where you'd never ever go? Why?	Is there **one place** where you'd never ever go? Why?

If you worked **in a circus**, would you be a lion tamer, an acrobat, or a clown, and why?	If you worked **in a circus**, would you be a lion tamer, an acrobat, or a clown, and why?	What is your **favorite TV** program?	What is your **favorite TV** program?
If you could collect anything, **what would you collect?**	If you could collect anything, **what would you collect?**	What would you describe as **a perfect Saturday?**	What would you describe as **a perfect Saturday?**
What habit do you have that you would most like to break?	**What habit** do you have that you would most like to break?	If you could **go back in time** to one place for one hour, where would you go?	If you could **go back in time** to one place for one hour, where would you go?
What's the **last book** you read, and did you like it?	What's the **last book** you read, and did you like it?	How do you feel about **surprise parties?**	How do you feel about **surprise parties?**
What is your all-time **favorite board game?**	What is your all-time **favorite board game?**	What one word do you think describes **being a good friend?**	What one word do you think describes **being a good friend?**

©/TM 2011 American Girl, LLC ©/TM 2011 American Girl, LLC ©/TM 2011 American Girl, LLC ©/TM 2011 American Girl, LLC

©/TM 2011 American Girl, LLC ©/TM 2011 American Girl, LLC ©/TM 2011 American Girl, LLC ©/TM 2011 American Girl, LLC

©/TM 2011 American Girl, LLC ©/TM 2011 American Girl, LLC ©/TM 2011 American Girl, LLC ©/TM 2011 American Girl, LLC

©/TM 2011 American Girl, LLC ©/TM 2011 American Girl, LLC ©/TM 2011 American Girl, LLC ©/TM 2011 American Girl, LLC

©/TM 2011 American Girl, LLC ©/TM 2011 American Girl, LLC ©/TM 2011 American Girl, LLC ©/TM 2011 American Girl, LLC

Brag Box

Keep a special box to store snapshots, mementos, artwork, report cards, and other stuff to show your grandma. After your grandma sees the contents of your box, store them elsewhere and start fresh for her next visit. Use an old hat box or cover a large papier-mâché box with nontoxic acrylic paint, let dry, and then attach decorative stickers.

Trade Secrets

Swap secret messages with your grandma. To encode a message, slip a secret word into every word you write. That way, if anyone glances at the message, it'll look like gibberish. To decode the message, cross out the secret word. Change the secret word with each new message.

Pass these sweet sayings to your grandma. Write each one on a mini gift card or around an envelope. See if your grandma can guess the secret word each time.

Code word: love

Thloveanks floveor makloveing mlovee feelovel sloveo lovloveed. Thloveere's nloveo plalovece oloven ealoverth lloveike yoloveur holoveuse.

Code word: treasure

Thtreasuree btreasureest ttreasurehings itreasuren liftreasuree aretreasuren't thintreasuregs— thtreasureey're grantreasuredmothers.

Code word: heart

Eveheartn iheartf Iheart didheartn't hheartave yheartou ahearts aheart grandmheartother, I'heartd chooheartse yheartou thearto bhearte mhearty frieheartnd.

Sweet Surprises

Tuck one of these little notes into your grandma's purse or pocket. Fold it in half, sign it, and seal it with a kiss.

1. Seven-letter
word for love

1. GRANDMA

Someone's
thinking about
you today.

ME!

S.W.A.K.
(Sealed with a kiss)

Gran
&
Me

To_____

From_____

©/TM 2011 American Girl, LLC

S.W.A.K.
(Sealed with a kiss)

Gran
&
Me

To_____

From_____

Take note:
I love you!

Presenting you with the
"Best Grandma Ever" Award

for

_____

_____

Gran
&
Me

To_____

From_____

Gran
&
Me

To_____

From_____

This note is

A HUG

from me to you.
Can you feel it?

Thanks for
being my

cheerleader!

S.W.A.K.
(Sealed with a kiss)

Gran & Me

To ____________________

From ____________________

©/TM 2011 American Girl, LLC

S.W.A.K.
(Sealed with a kiss)

Gran & Me

To ____________________

From ____________________

Smile!

Somebody loves you.

(Guess who?)

Today
I thought of you.

S.W.A.K.
(Sealed with a kiss)

Gran & Me

To_______________________

From_____________________

©/TM 2011 American Girl, LLC

S.W.A.K.
(Sealed with a kiss)

Gran & Me

To_______________________

From_____________________

Your Go-To Girl!

Need ideas for a class project? Want help dealing with a conflict? Like hearing funny stories about a parent or relative? Talk to your grandma! This go-to gal might have the wisdom you need for almost any situation. So keep her at the top of your BFF list!

Would you rather . . .

eat pizza or pasta? Live in the past or in the future? Take turns answering each question with your grandma. If you disagree, talk about why.

Would you rather . . .

. . . color in a coloring book or draw your own art to color?

. . . sail in the ocean or swim in a pool?

. . . try to cure diseases or try to solve crimes?

. . . sleep in a room with one big hairy spider or a room with 100 flies?

. . . have a job creating new ice-cream flavors or inventing new board games?

. . . be a butterfly and live in a garden or be a bird and live in the trees?

. . . see fireworks or see a meteor shower?

. . . act in a Hollywood movie or sing a chart-topping song?

Fun + Food

Eat a memorable meal with your grandma! Picnic at a park. Dine in the den. Bring takeout to the top of a scenic hill. Pack a picnic basket, bring a quilt, and take photos of your special time.

Puzzle Post

Have some really good news to send to your grandma? Build up her anticipation with a puzzle! Write the news on card-stock paper, add art or designs, and cut it up into puzzle pieces. Then mail the pieces to your grandma. Write "Breaking News" on the back of the envelope.

Family Favorites

Can you guess your grandma's favorite things? Can she guess yours? And how much do you have in common?

Tear out the lists, and give one to your grandma to fill out.

Me

	Mine	Grandma's
• Favorite flower		
• Favorite jelly-bean flavor		
• Favorite smell		
• Favorite charity		
• Favorite milk shake		
• Favorite type of shoe		
• Favorite sound		
• Favorite clothing item		
• Favorite soup		
• Favorite holiday		
• Favorite word		

Grandma

	Mine	Grand-daughter's
• Favorite flower		
• Favorite jelly-bean flavor		
• Favorite smell		
• Favorite charity		
• Favorite milk shake		
• Favorite type of shoe		
• Favorite sound		
• Favorite clothing item		
• Favorite soup		
• Favorite holiday		
• Favorite word		

Stories of Stuff

Make a memory by asking your grandmother about the history behind some of her favorite keepsakes. Where did she get her Italian cameo necklace? Why does she treasure the antique quilt on her bed? Who earned the old trophies she displays in the family room? If you like, share some of the stories about your own stuff.

Pass the Popcorn!

Give your grandma a special treat with tongue-tickling popcorn flavors. Fill a tin (or a bag) with the popcorn, and attach a label for the flavor you created. Hand deliver the special treat, or slip it in a box and send it to your grandma. Send her one flavor at a time, a couple of flavors mixed together, or all of the flavors at once!

Tear out the label for the flavor you make, and glue it to your gift tin or bag.

Pick a popcorn! Pour 6 cups of popped old-fashioned or plain microwaved popcorn into a bag. Add a mix-in, seal, and shake.

Cheese Pleaser
2 tablespoons powdered
cheese topping

Kettle Korn
¼ cup sugar plus
½ teaspoon cinnamon

Tex Mex
1 teaspoon taco seasoning plus
2 tablespoons powdered
cheese topping

Movie Madness
1 cup Milk Duds

Peanut Butter Cup
½ cup chocolate chips plus
½ cup peanut butter chips

Pucker Popper
1 teaspoon dry ranch dressing mix

Cheese Pleaser

Popcorn made
with love by me!

Kettle Korn

Popcorn made
with love by me!

Tex Mex

Popcorn made
with love by me!

Movie Madness

Popcorn made
with love by me!

Pucker Popper

Popcorn made
with love by me!

Peanut Butter Cup

Popcorn made
with love by me!

Sweet Perfume

Create edible perfume bottles with grandma. Look for hard candies in different shapes and colors. Use a toothpick to dab icing on the candies to help the pieces stick together. Display the sweets—or eat them up!

Music Magic

Ask someone (other than your grandma) to help you make a CD of songs that your grandma liked when she was your age. Every year for your grandma's birthday, create a new CD to add to her music collection.

Tear out one of these covers, fill in the playlist on the back, and slide the cover into the front of a CD case.

Grand Tunes!

To: _____

From: _____

Date: _____

A Blast from the Past

To: _____

From: _____

Date: _____

Sofa Stories

Ask your grandmother if she can show you a family photo album, and then curl up on the couch for some good stories. That little girl with the funny hairdo might be your mother!

Tear-&-Share Coupons

Give your grandma the gift of special time with you. Tear out one of these coupons, and tuck it into a card for her. Ask her to recycle the coupons by giving them back to you someday.

Have a Hug

*

This coupon is good for one big bear hug.

Funny Face

*

This coupon is good for a silly face
to make you smile.

Snack Saver

*

This coupon is good for a treat made by me.

Game Day

*

This coupon is good for one game of anything you'd like to play.

Walk & Talk

*

This coupon is good for a relaxing walk. Pick the time, and I'll walk with you.

U Choose

*

This coupon is good for 30 minutes of together time. You pick the activity.

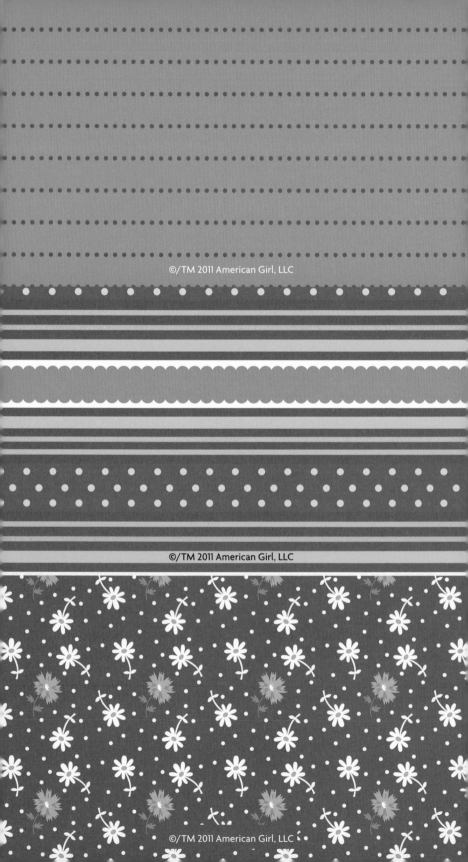

Future Fun

You and your grandma write down your predictions for the next month. They can be about anything—the outcome of a TV show, who in the family will earn good grades or win a sporting event, or even what a parent will serve for a particular meal. Slip the predictions in a box or bag and seal it until the time has passed. Who had the best powers of prediction?

Nightie Night

Use these door hangers on the INSIDE of your room to remind you that someone special is thinking about you.

Pull out the door hangers, and give one to your grandma. Punch out the perforated circles before sliding the hangers onto doorknobs.

Carefully punch out
along dotted lines.

Carefully punch out
along dotted lines.

Good night,
sleep tight,
wishing
you sweet
dreams
tonight.

Good night,
sleep tight,
wishing
you sweet
dreams
tonight.

Somebody
special
really
loves
me.

Somebody
special
really
loves
me.

Picture Day!

Every day for a week, take a
picture of (or draw) something
that makes you feel happy. Ask
your grandma to do the same.
When the week's over, trade
your images and talk
about them. What did
you discover?

Book Buddies

Look for books you and your grandma can share and discuss. Take turns picking books to read and review.

Tear out a bookmark and give one to your grandma. Each time you read a book, write it on a line, and fill in the number of stars you'd give it.

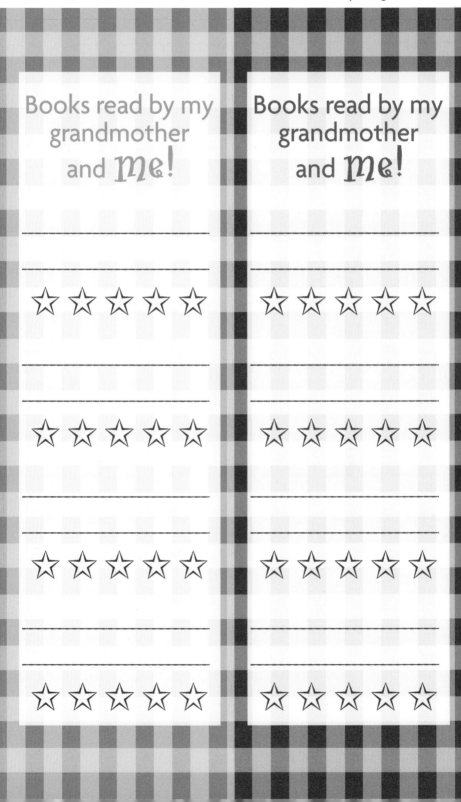

Seesaw Stories

Read one of these story starters out loud to your grandma. Take turns adding sentences to the story until one of you declares "the end."

"Mouse-flavored cereal?" said Grandma. "Why would you ask for that for breakfast?" (Your name here) looked over at the cat. "But *I* didn't."

"Why do you keep that *thing?*" (Your name here) asked her grandma. "It's scary and it smells." Her grandmother replied, "If you must know . . ."

"He's here!" (your name here) shouted to her grandmother. The two darted onto the porch and gasped when they saw that "he" was . . .

"What was it like to be the first travelers to Planet Gorg?" the reporter asked. "Well," (your name here) said, looking at her grandma, "we saw . . ."

"They'd better not catch us!" (your name here)'s grandmother said as the two ducked behind a Dumpster. "Because if they do . . ."

Jar of Fun

When you think of something you'd like to do with your grandma, write it on a slip of paper. Ask her to do the same. Toss your ideas into a clean, empty jar. When you have time together, pull out an idea and give it a try!

Start your jar with the ideas on the next page, and then add some of your own.

create a list of as many ice cream flavors as you can	create a comic strip about the two of you
decorate a pair of cool rocks with stickers	start a collection
make tissue-paper flowers for friends and family	invent a new tradition for your next holiday
draw your dream houses	do each other's hair
give each other shoulder massages	put together a jigsaw puzzle
do yoga	show each other dances you like to do
talk about the day you were born	toss rolled socks into a bucket—first to ten wins
deliver food to a food pantry	cook a meal together for your family
make seasonal decorations	copy a word search—see who finds the words first

Jar of Fun

©/TM 2011 American Girl, LLC

Jar of Fun

©/TM 2011 American Girl, LLC

Jar of Fun

©/TM 2011 American Girl, LLC

Jar of Fun

©/TM 2011 American Girl, LLC

Jar of Fun

©/TM 2011 American Girl, LLC

Jar of Fun

©/TM 2011 American Girl, LLC

Jar of Fun

©/TM 2011 American Girl, LLC

Jar of Fun

©/TM 2011 American Girl, LLC

Jar of Fun

©/TM 2011 American Girl, LLC

Jar of Fun

©/TM 2011 American Girl, LLC

Jar of Fun

©/TM 2011 American Girl, LLC

Jar of Fun

©/TM 2011 American Girl, LLC

Jar of Fun

©/TM 2011 American Girl, LLC

Jar of Fun

©/TM 2011 American Girl, LLC

Jar of Fun

©/TM 2011 American Girl, LLC

Jar of Fun

©/TM 2011 American Girl, LLC

Your Turn!

Start a project that the two of you can add to on your own. Send it or hand it back and forth until it's done.

- Choose a big subject, such as a carnival, and start a sketch. Add to the art until your page is packed!

- Make a monthly calendar. You fill in your sporting events or activities and your grandma fills in her schedule.

- Share an acrostic poem. Choose a word, such as "summer." Take turns writing a word for each letter.

- Write a story—you create the dialogue for one character and your grandma writes dialogue for the other.

- Color a giant art poster together. Color until you're tired, and then pass it on.

Love Letters

Everyone loves mail, so even if you live in the same town as your grandmother, send her a letter. To get started, tear out the stationery at right, and write a letter. Fill out the hearts, and then pop them up before passing the letter on.

Dear

_____,

Love,

_____

Love Around the World

Surprise your grandma by telling her "I love you" in different languages.

In:	"I love you" is:
French	*Je t'aime (zheh tem)*
German	*Ich liebe dich (eekh LEE-beh deekh)*
Italian	*Ti amo (tee AH-mo)*
Japanese	*Ai shiteru (eye she-tuh-roo)*
Mandarin Chinese	*wo ai ni (wah eye nee)*
Spanish	Te amo (teh AH-moh)

Kooky Competitions

Just for laughs, challenge your grandma to some silly games. Use the ones on the right page, and then make up your own. Pass out mini certificates to the winners!

House of Cards

Divide a deck of cards, and each take half. On "Go!," you have 1 minute to build a house with your cards. After time's up, count the cards you each have STANDING. The one with the most wins!

It's a Wrap!

You'll need two dice, two 2-by-3-inch pieces of wrapping paper, and tape. On "Go!," be the first to wrap a die until it looks like a mini package.

Twisted Lips

See who can repeat this tongue twister the most times in 1 minute without messing up:

A chatty chicken chef chirps as she shaves cheddar cheese slices in the cramped kitchen.

Measure Up

You'll need a ball of yarn and scissors. Choose an object, such as a ball—but don't touch it. Each of you cuts a piece of yarn that you think will fit perfectly around that object. Now measure. Try another object. The one with the most wins in 5 tries is the champ!

Card Champion

Awarded to:

_____

Wrapping Winner

Awarded to:

_____

Twister Titleholder

Awarded to:

_____

Measuring Medalist

Awarded to:

_____

Secret Signs

Come up with a signal that only the two of you will understand. Blinking three times might mean "I love you." Two tugs on your ear might mean "Let's go." What other silly signs can you think of?

Make a Pact

This book is ending, but the good times with your grandma will go on and on. Sign this pact and post it on the fridge to remind yourselves to stay connected and to make time for fun.

Our Pact

We vow to:

- make the most of our time together,

- set up one-on-one dates as often as we can, and

- laugh together.

Signed:

_____
(me)

and

_____
(my grandma)

Date: _____

Which grandma-and-me
quizzes, games, and activities
did you like best? What are your
favorite things to do with
your grandma?

Write to us!

Just Grandma and Me Editor
American Girl
8400 Fairway Place
Middleton, WI 53562

(All comments and suggestions
received by American Girl may be used
without compensation or acknowledgment.
Sorry—photos can't be returned.)

Here are some other American Girl books you might like:

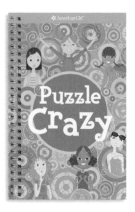

❑ *I read it.*

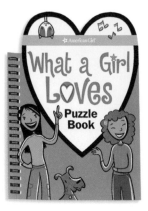

❑ *I read it.*

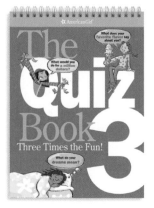

❑ *I read it.*

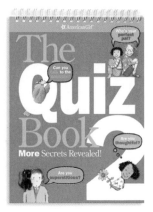

❑ *I read it.*

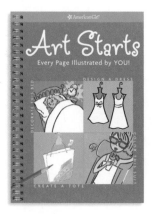

❑ *I read it.*

❑ *I read it.*